The GREEDY Triangle

With thanks to Jim Robertson and Tom Schneider
for inspiring this story. —M.B.
For Merle. —G.S.

Marilyn Burns Brainy Day Books is a trademark of Marilyn Burns
Education Associates.

24 23 22 21 20 19 18 17 16   0/0 01 02

Printed in the U.S.A.

*The illustrations in this book were
done in acrylic airbrush and colored
pencils on bristol board.*

Library of Congress Cataloging-in-Publication Data

Burns, Marilyn, 1941–
    The greedy triangle / by Marilyn Burns; illustrated by Gordon Silveria.
        p.   cm.
    "A Marilyn Burns brainy day book."
    Summary: Dissatisfied with its shape, a triangle keeps asking the local shape-
shifter to add more lines and angles until it doesn't know which side is up.
    ISBN 0-590-48991-7
    [1. Shape—Fiction.   2. Self-acceptance—Fiction.]
I. Silveria, Gordon, ill.   II. Title.
PZ7.B93739Gr 1994
[E]—dc20   94-11308
                            CIP
                            AC

The GREEDY Triangle

WRITTEN BY MARILYN BURNS

ILLUSTRATED BY GORDON SILVERIA

A Marilyn Burns Brainy Day Book

SCHOLASTIC INC. ♦ NEW YORK

Once there was a triangle that was—as most triangles are—always busy.

The triangle spent its time holding up roofs,

supporting bridges,

making music in a symphony orchestra,

catching the wind for sailboats,

being slices of pie and halves of sandwiches,

and much, much more.

The triangle's favorite thing, however, was to slip into place when people put their hands on their hips. "That way I always hear the latest news," it said, "which I can tell my friends."

The triangle's friends liked hearing the news.

One day, the triangle began to feel dissatisfied. "I'm tired of doing the same old things," it grumbled. "There must be more to life." So the triangle went to see the local shapeshifter.

"How may I help you?" the shapeshifter asked the triangle.

"I think if I had just one more side and one more angle," said the triangle, "my life would be more interesting."

"That's easy to do," said the shapeshifter.

Poof! The shapeshifter turned the triangle into a quadrilateral.

Life changed in a wonderful way. The quadrilateral was happy with all the new things it could do.

The quadrilateral could be a baseball diamond, or first, second, or third base.

It could take a position on a checkerboard or a chessboard.

It could be a television screen, a computer screen, or a movie screen.

It could frame windows or frame pictures, and much, much more.

The quadrilateral's favorite thing, however, was to be the pages of a book. "I learn so many interesting stories that way," it said, "which I can tell my friends."

The quadrilateral's friends liked hearing the stories.

But one day, the quadrilateral began to feel dissatisfied. "I'm tired of doing the same old things," it grumbled. "There must be more to life." So the quadrilateral went back to the shapeshifter.

"How may I help you now?" the shapeshifter asked the quadrilateral.

"I think if I had just one more side and one more angle," said the quadrilateral, "my life would be more interesting."

"That's easy to do," said the shapeshifter.

Poof! The shapeshifter turned the quadrilateral into a pentagon.

Life changed in a wonderful way. The pentagon was happy with all the new things it could do.

On a baseball diamond, the pentagon could be home plate.

It could be a section on a soccer ball,

or appear inside whenever someone drew a five-pointed star.

The pentagon's favorite thing, however, was to be the headquarters of the United States military near Washington, D.C. "I hear all the top secrets that way," it said. "It's too bad I can't tell them to my friends." The pentagon's friends couldn't help feeling left out.

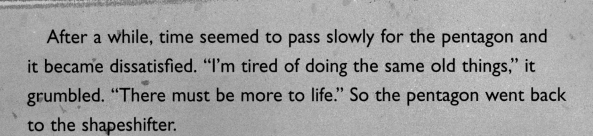

After a while, time seemed to pass slowly for the pentagon and it became dissatisfied. "I'm tired of doing the same old things," it grumbled. "There must be more to life." So the pentagon went back to the shapeshifter.

"So, you're here again," the shapeshifter said to the pentagon. "Now what would you like?"

"I think if I had just one more side and one more angle," said the pentagon, "my life would be more interesting."

"That's easy to do," said the shapeshifter.

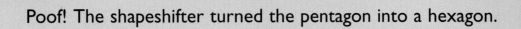

Poof! The shapeshifter turned the pentagon into a hexagon.

Life changed again in a wonderful way. The hexagon was happy with all the new things it could do.

The hexagon fit in as floor tiles in houses and patios and fancy crackers at parties and picnics.

It worked as the socket of certain bolts and the prongs of certain wrenches.

The hexagon's favorite thing, however, was to be a cell in a beehive. "I love watching the bees as they buzz in and out," it said. The hexagon spent so much time in the beehive, it was too busy to talk to its friends. The friends missed the hexagon and couldn't help feeling ignored.

Again and again, the shape became restless, dissatisfied, and unhappy with its life. Again and again, it returned to the shapeshifter for more sides and more angles. The shapeshifter agreed to turn it into one shape after another.

A heptagon,

an octagon,

a nonagon,

a decagon,

and on and on.

Finally, the shape had many, many sides and many, many angles. Its sides were so small that it had trouble keeping its balance. Its friends couldn't tell which side it was on and began to avoid the shape.

One day, when the shape was going down a hill, it began to roll. Faster and faster it went, screeching around corners, crashing into fences and trees, colliding with bicycles, and terrifying walkers.

At last, the shape came to a stop. It felt tired and dizzy, lonely and sad.

"Enough," thought the shape. "I don't know which side is up. I can't keep my balance. My friends don't want me around." The shape could no longer remember why it had been so unhappy as a triangle. Very carefully, it made its way back to the shapeshifter.

"Aren't you happy yet?" the shapeshifter asked.

"I want to be a triangle again," said the shape.

"I'm not surprised," said the shapeshifter.

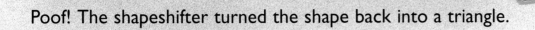

Poof! The shapeshifter turned the shape back into a triangle.

The triangle was delighted to have its old shape back again and kept itself very busy.

Once again, it held up roofs,

supported bridges,

made music in a symphony orchestra,

caught the wind for sailboats,

became slices of pie and halves of sandwiches,

and much, much more.

Still, the triangle's favorite thing was to slip into place when people put their hands on their hips. "That way I always hear the latest news," it said, "which I can tell my friends."

Its friends liked hearing the news and were glad the triangle was back in shape again.

For Parents, Teachers, and Other Adults

Before they enter school, young children have had considerable experience with geometry from investigating, playing, and building with shapes. *The Greedy Triangle* contributes to children's learning by presenting shapes in a combination of real-world and imaginary contexts. The story invites children to wonder about what happens to shapes as they get more sides and more angles and introduces children to the names of the polygons.

About the Mathematics

From their early experiences, children often develop particular or favorite ways to think about shapes. For example, children often picture triangles in the same position, with one angle pointing up. It's not uncommon for a child to describe a triangle drawn in another position as being "upside-down" or "sideways" and, therefore, somehow wrong. Similarly, when a square is drawn with sides parallel to the edge of a paper, it is clearly a square to children. But if a square is drawn on a tilt, children will often insist that it's a diamond, not a square. One of the benefits of *The Greedy Triangle* is that it shows shapes in many different forms and positions and places them in contexts that make them accessible to children. The illustrations give children a chance to think more flexibly about shapes and how they are used.

Also, the book introduces the correct names for geometric shapes. Common geometric names used —triangle, square, rectangle, for example—are easy for children to learn. Other words—quadrilateral, pentagon, hexagon, for example—are not as familiar, to adults or children. While the focus of children's learning should be on understanding, not on terminology, it's helpful for adults to have some background information. Here's a primer.

The Greedy Triangle is all about polygons, shapes with sides that are straight line segments. A formal definition of polygon is that it is "a closed plane figure bound by three or more straight line segments." The "closed" part means that it encloses a space, like a fence around a corral. The "plane" part means it's on a flat surface. Polygons are named for the number of sides they have:

3 sides	= triangle	8 sides	= octagon
4 sides	= quadrilateral	9 sides	= nonagon
5 sides	= pentagon	10 sides	= decagon
6 sides	= hexagon	11 sides	= undecagon
7 sides	= heptagon	12 sides	= dodecagon

Also, although every four-sided polygon is a quadrilateral, some quadrilaterals are more commonly known by other names—square, rectangle, parallelogram, rhombus, or trapezoid. The name that's used depends on the context, just as someone can be called Mrs. Greene or Deborah or Mom, depending on the particular situation. As with all new vocabulary, children learn geometry words best when they hear them used in different ways and are encouraged to use them.

A circle is not a polygon. That's because its sides are not straight line segments. As a matter of fact, it doesn't have sides, but is "a closed plane figure bound by a curve, every point on which is the same distance from the center of the circle." As a polygon gets more and more sides, it starts to look more circle-like; its sides become smaller and its angles become larger. Mathematicians say it "approaches" being a circle, shown in *The Greedy Triangle* as the polygon begins to roll.

Extending Children's Learning

To stimulate children's thinking during and after reading the story, try the following:

1. Put your hands on your hips and have a child trace the triangle inside your arms. Have children explain how they are sure when a shape is a triangle.

2. Ask children to imagine what the triangle will become with one more side and one more angle. Have them predict for other shapes as well. Children may respond with real-life examples instead of names of shapes. For example, a child might say that a quadrilateral would turn into a house. A response such as, "Yes, a house is an example of a pentagon" accepts the child's answer and also uses correct geometric language.

3. Take a walk to look for shapes in the real world. Focus on just one shape, such as a triangle, or search for examples of all shapes. To help children keep track of their ideas, give them paper on a clipboard or make a small blank book by cutting plain paper in half and stapling several sheets together. Have children draw what they see and, if they can, write something to remind them what and where it was.

4. Ask children their ideas about why a shape with many sides and many angles, like a dodecagon, would roll more easily than a shape with fewer sides and angles, like a triangle or quadrilateral. The purpose of the question isn't to elicit a right answer, but to stimulate children's thinking about shapes.

5. Suggest an art activity. Cut out an assortment of polygons in several colors. Have children choose one and think about what it might be a part of. When they have an idea, they glue the shape to a piece of white drawing paper and draw a picture around it.

While there is mathematical content in *The Greedy Triangle*, keep in mind that the book is meant to engage and delight children, stimulate their imaginations, and encourage them to develop a love of books and reading. As with any book, invite children's reactions. Some children may interrupt the story to express an idea or ask a question. Some may want to talk about the illustrations. Others may listen intently until the end. All of these reactions are fine. At all times, follow the child's lead.